——— Words of ———
FRIENDSHIP

To Ellen
From S. Marie
with love

Original edition published in English under the title
Words of Friendship by Lion Publishing, Tring, England,
copyright © 1983 Lion Publishing.

First published in the United States and Canada in
1983 by Thomas Nelson Publishers.

Published in Nashville, Tennessee, by Thomas Nelson,
Inc. and distributed in Canada by Lawson Falle, Ltd.,
Cambridge, Ontario.

Photographs by Robin Bath, pages 15, 25 and cover; John
Cleare/Mountain Camera, page 31; Sister Daniel, pages 7,
13, 29; Fritz Fankhauser, page 27; Lion Publishing/David
Alexander, pages 21, 23, 33, 37, 39; David Vesey, page 35;
Jon Willcocks, pages 9, 11, 17, 19, 41, 43, 45

Scripture quotations are from the *Good News Bible*—Old
Testament: Copyright © American Bible Society 1976;
New Testament: Copyright © American Bible Society
1966, 1971, 1976.

ISBN 0-8407-5334-9

Words of
FRIENDSHIP

Thomas Nelson Publishers
Nashville • Camden • New York

THE FRIENDSHIP OF GOD

The Lord is the friend of those who obey him
and he affirms his covenant with them.
I look to the Lord for help at all times,
and he rescues me from danger.
Turn to me, Lord, and be merciful to me,
because I am lonely and weak.
Relieve me of my worries and save me from all
my troubles.
Consider my distress and suffering
and forgive all my sins.

PSALM 25:14–18

GOD'S LOVE FOR HIS PEOPLE

The Lord says,
"When Israel was a child, I loved him
and called him out of Egypt as my son.
But the more I called to him,
the more he turned away from me.
My people sacrificed to Baal;
they burnt incense to idols.
Yet I was the one who taught Israel to walk.
I took my people up in my arms,
but they did not acknowledge that I
took care of them.
I drew them to me with affection and love.
I picked them up and held them to my cheek;
I bent down to them and fed them."

HOSEA 11:1–4

"I WILL TRUST HIM"

A day is coming when people will sing,
"I praise you, Lord! You were angry with me,
but now you comfort me and are angry no
longer.
God is my savior; I will trust him and not be
afraid.
The Lord gives me power and strength;
he is my savior.
As fresh water brings joy to the thirsty,
so God's people rejoice when he saves them."

ISAIAH 12:1–3

THE FRIEND OF GOD

How was our ancestor Abraham put right with God? It was through his actions, when he offered his son Isaac on the altar. Can't you see? His faith and his actions worked together; his faith was made perfect through his actions. And the scripture came true that said, "Abraham believed God, and because of his faith God accepted him as righteous." And so Abraham was called God's friend. You see, then, that it is by his actions that a person is put right with God, and not by his faith alone.

JAMES 2:21–24

NO LONGER ENEMIES

At one time you were far away from God and were his enemies because of the evil things you did and thought. But now, by means of the physical death of his Son, God has made you his friends, in order to bring you, holy, pure, and faultless, into his presence.

COLOSSIANS 1:21–22

I CALL YOU FRIENDS

Jesus said:
"My commandment is this: love one another, just as I love you. The greatest love a person can have for his friends is to give his life for them. And you are my friends if you do what I command you. I do not call you servants any longer, because a servant does not know what his master is doing. Instead, I call you friends, because I have told you everything I heard from my Father . . . This, then, is what I command you: love one another."

JOHN 15:12–15, 17

"THE GREATEST IS LOVE . . ."

The people reply:
"But he endured the suffering that should have
been ours,
the pain that we should have borne.
All the while we thought that his suffering
was punishment sent by God.
But because of our sins he was wounded,
beaten because of the evil we did.
We are healed by the punishment he suffered,
made whole by the blows he received.
All of us were like sheep that were lost,
each of us going his own way.
But the Lord made the punishment fall on him,
the punishment all of us deserved."

ISAIAH 53:4–6

WHAT GOD HAS DONE

It is a difficult thing for someone to die for a righteous person . . . But God has shown us how much he loves us—it was while we were still sinners that Christ died for us! By his sacrificial death we are now put right with God; how much more, then, will we be saved by him from God's anger! We were God's enemies, but he made us his friends through the death of his Son. Now that we are God's friends, how much more will we be saved by Christ's life! But that is not all; we rejoice because of what God has done through our Lord Jesus Christ, who has now made us God's friends.

ROMANS 5:7–11

LASTING FRIENDSHIPS

Some friendships do not last, but some friends are more loyal than brothers.

PROVERBS 18:24

DAVID AND JONATHAN

Saul's son Jonathan . . . came to love [David] as much as he loved himself. Saul kept David with him from that day on and did not let him go back home. Jonathan swore eternal friendship with David because of his deep affection for him.

1 SAMUEL 18:1–3

TRUE LOYALTY

Ruth answered:
"Don't ask me to leave you! Let me go with you.
Wherever you go, I will go; wherever you live, I
will live. Your people will be my people, and
your God will be my God. Wherever you die, I
will die, and that is where I will be buried. May
the Lord's worst punishment come upon me if I
let anything but death separate me from you!"

RUTH 1:16–17

JESUS' LOVE FOR LAZARUS

Mary arrived where Jesus was, and as soon as she saw him, she fell at his feet. "Lord," she said, "if you had been here, my brother would not have died!"
Jesus saw her weeping, and he saw how the people who were with her were weeping also; his heart was touched, and he was deeply moved. "Where have you buried him?" he asked them.
"Come and see, Lord," they answered. Jesus wept.
"See how much he loved him!" the people said.

JOHN 11:32–35

TRUE FRIENDS

I recommend to you our sister Phoebe, who serves the church at Cenchreae. Receive her in the Lord's name, as God's people should, and give her any help she may need from you; for she herself has been a good friend to many people and also to me.
I send greetings to Priscilla and Aquila, my fellow workers in the service of Christ Jesus; they risked their lives for me. I am grateful to them—not only I, but all the Gentile churches as well.

ROMANS 16:1–4

JESUS—FRIEND OF SINNERS

There was a chief tax collector there named
Zacchaeus, who was rich. He was trying to see
who Jesus was, but he was a little man and could
not see Jesus because of the crowd. So he ran
ahead of the crowd and climbed a sycamore tree
to see Jesus, who was going to pass that way.
When Jesus came to that place, he looked up and
said to Zacchaeus, "Hurry down, Zacchaeus,
because I must stay in your house today."
Zacchaeus hurried down and welcomed him with
great joy. All the people who saw it started
grumbling, "This man has gone as a guest to the
home of a sinner!"
Zacchaeus stood up and said to the Lord,
"Listen, sir! I will give half my belongings to the
poor, and if I have cheated anyone, I will pay
him back four times as much."
Jesus said to him, "Salvation has come to this
house today, for this man, also, is a descendant
of Abraham. The Son of Man came to seek and
to save the lost."

LUKE 19:2–10

FRIENDSHIPS TO AVOID

Don't make friends with people who have hot,
violent tempers. You might learn their habits and
not be able to change.

PROVERBS 22:24–25

A FRIEND IN NEED

Jesus answered:
"There was once a man who was going down
from Jerusalem to Jericho when robbers attacked
him, stripped him, and beat him up, leaving him
half dead . . .
But a Samaritan who was travelling that way
came upon the man, and when he saw him, his
heart was filled with pity. He went over to him,
poured oil and wine on his wounds and
bandaged them; then he put the man on his own
animal and took him to an inn, where he took
care of him. The next day he took out two silver
coins and gave them to the innkeeper. 'Take care
of him', he told the innkeeper, 'and when I come
back this way, I will pay you whatever else you
spend on him.'"

And Jesus concluded, "In your opinion, which
one of these three acted like a neighbor towards
the man attacked by the robbers?"
The teacher of the Law answered, "The one who
was kind to him."
Jesus replied, "You go, then, and do the same."

LUKE 10:30, 33–37

SOUND ADVICE

A friend means well, even when he hurts you.
But when an enemy puts his arm round your
shoulder—watch out!

PROVERBS 27:6

TEST OF FRIENDSHIP

Peter came to Jesus and asked, "Lord, if my brother keeps on sinning against me, how many times do I have to forgive him? Seven times?" "No, not seven times," answered Jesus, "but seventy times seven."

MATTHEW 18:21–22

RELATIONSHIPS WITH OTHERS

But the Spirit produces love, joy, peace, patience,
kindness, goodness, faithfulness, humility, and
self-control. There is no law against such things
as these. And those who belong to Christ Jesus
have put to death their human nature with all its
passions and desires. The Spirit has given us life;
he must also control our lives. We must not be
proud or irritate one another or be jealous of one
another.

GALATIANS 5:22–26

FORGIVE ONE ANOTHER

You are the people of God; he loved you and chose you for his own. So then, you must clothe yourselves with compassion, kindness, humility, gentleness, and patience. Be tolerant with one another and forgive one another whenever any of you has a complaint against someone else. You must forgive one another just as the Lord has forgiven you. And to all these qualities add love, which binds all things together in perfect unity.

COLOSSIANS 3:12–14